This Coloring
Books
Belongs To :

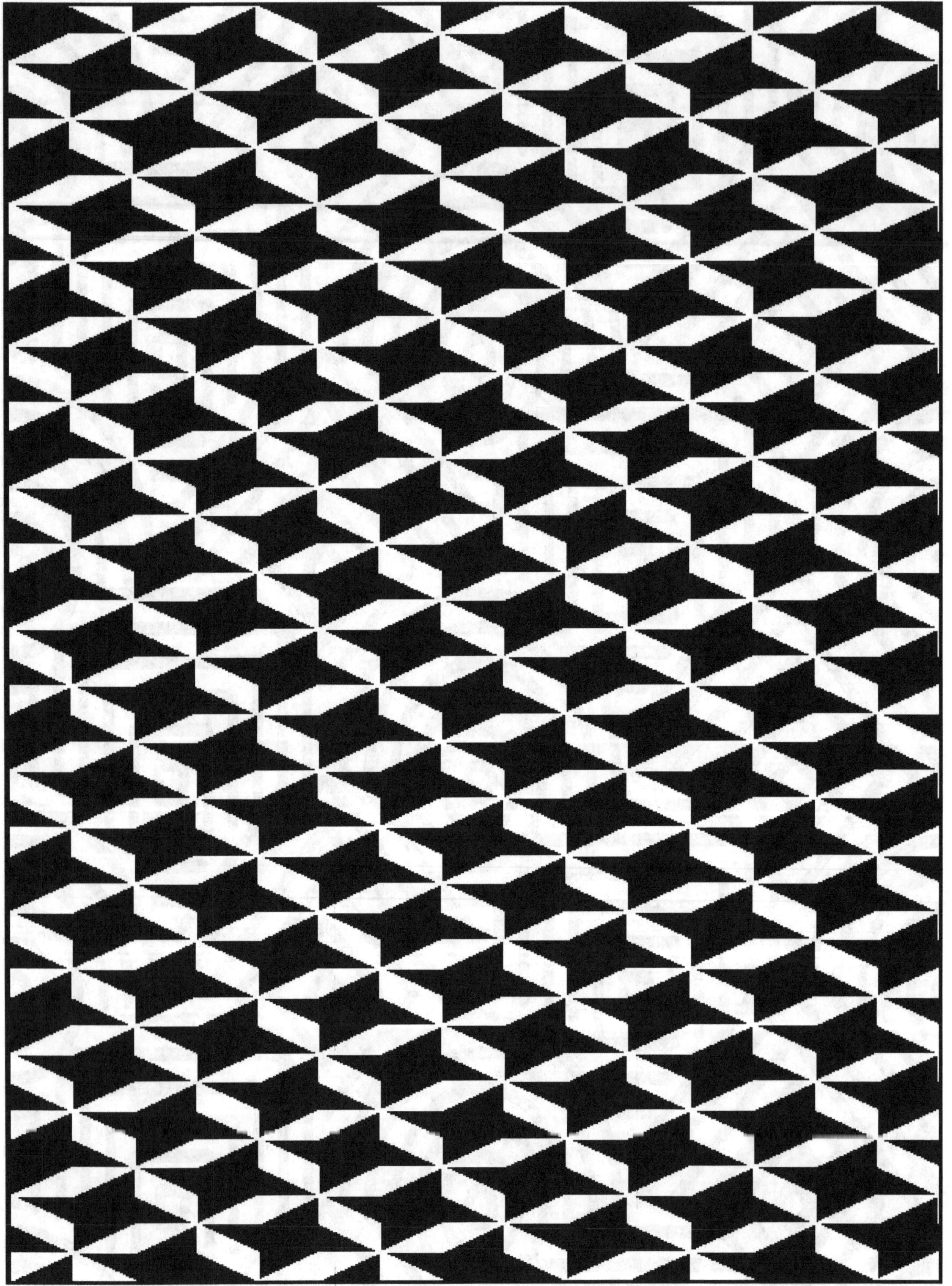

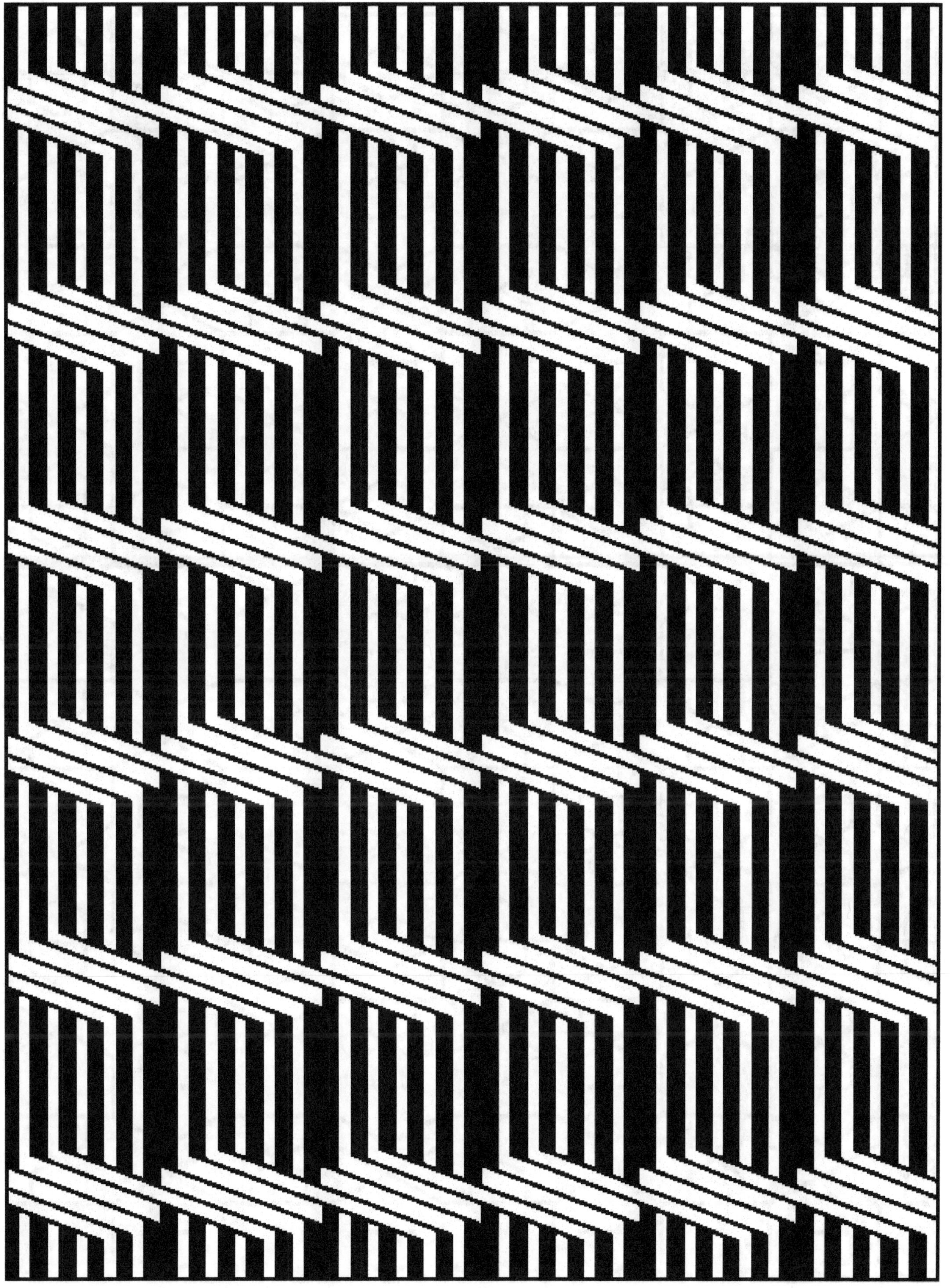

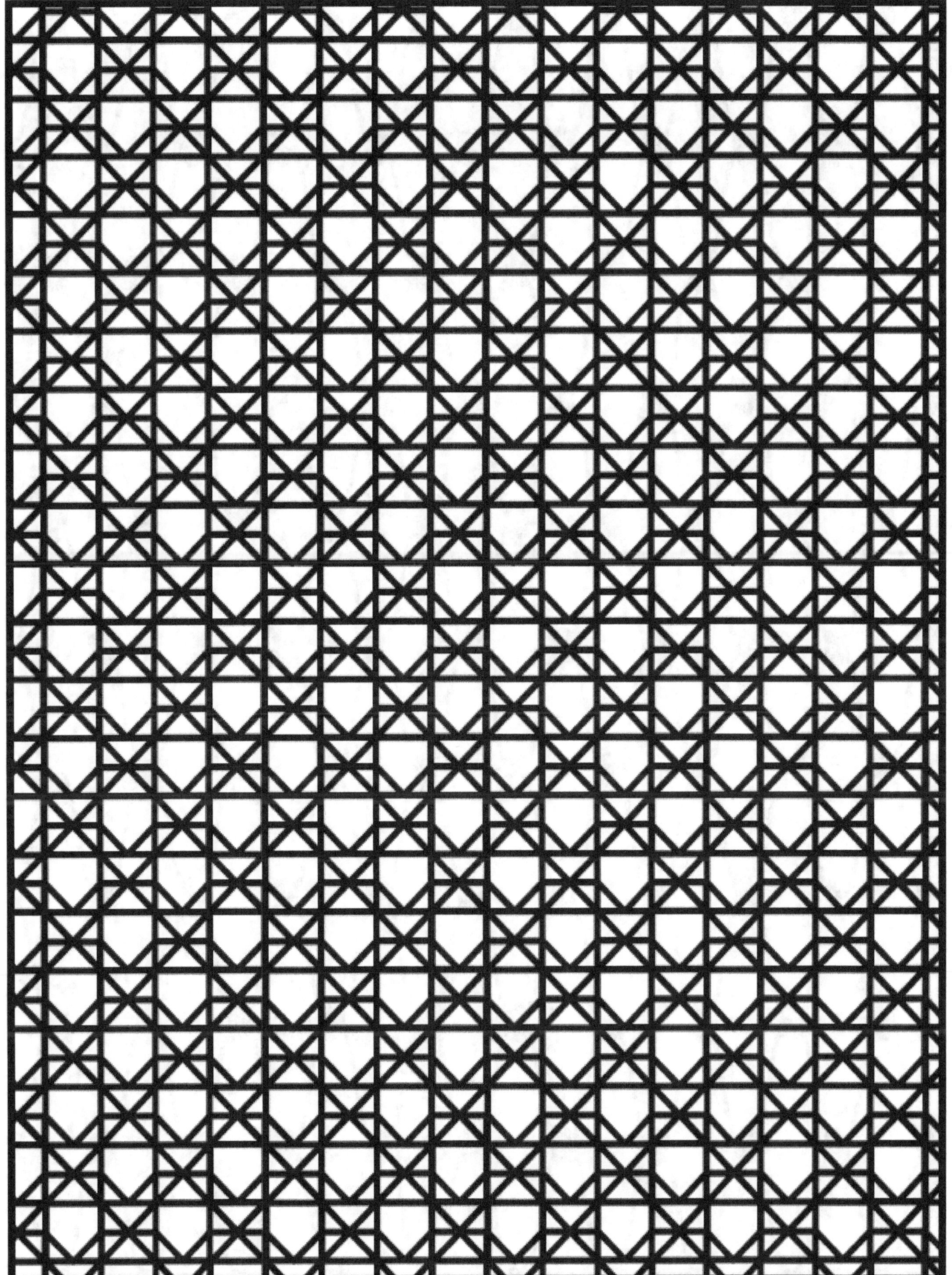

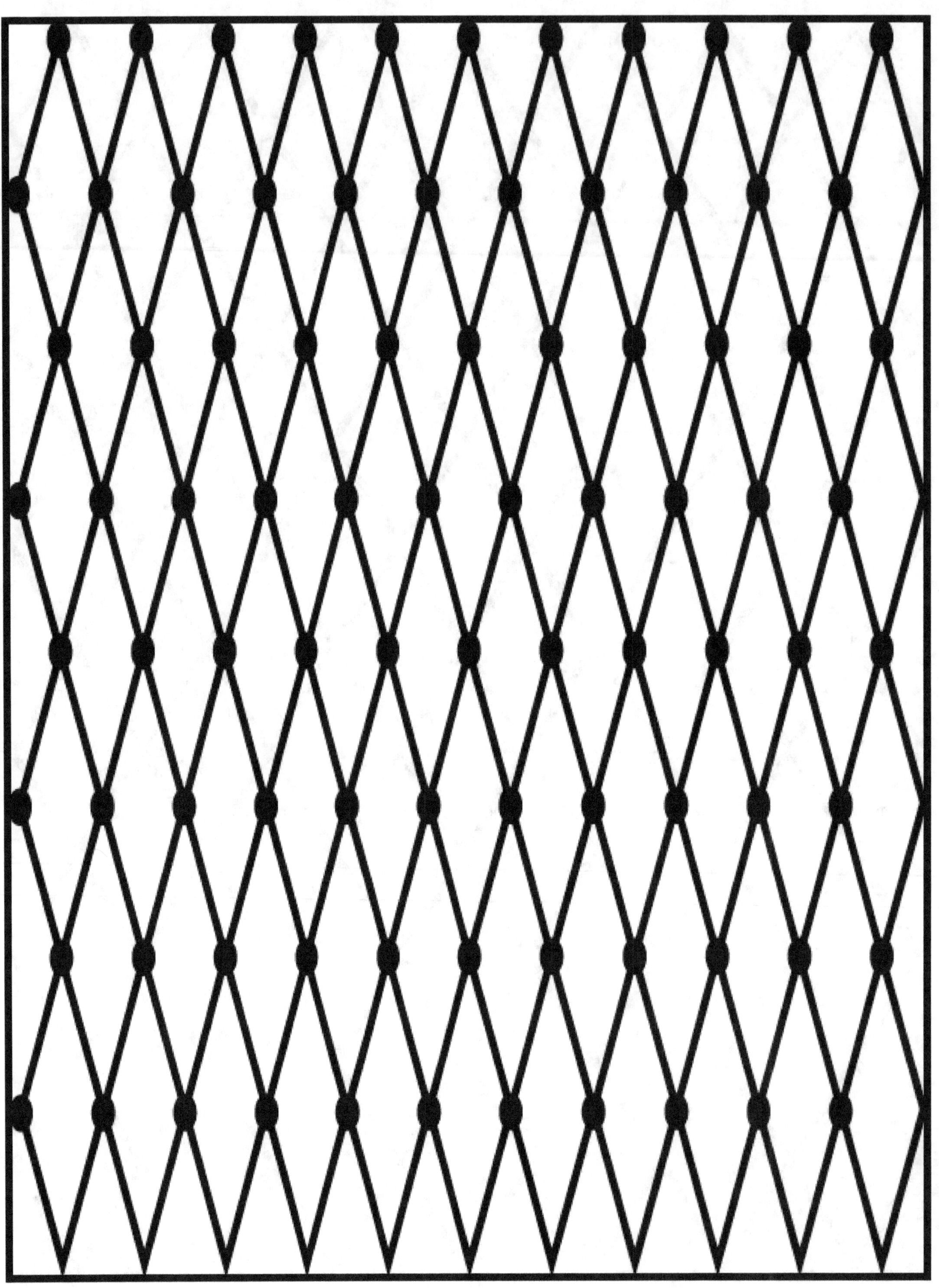

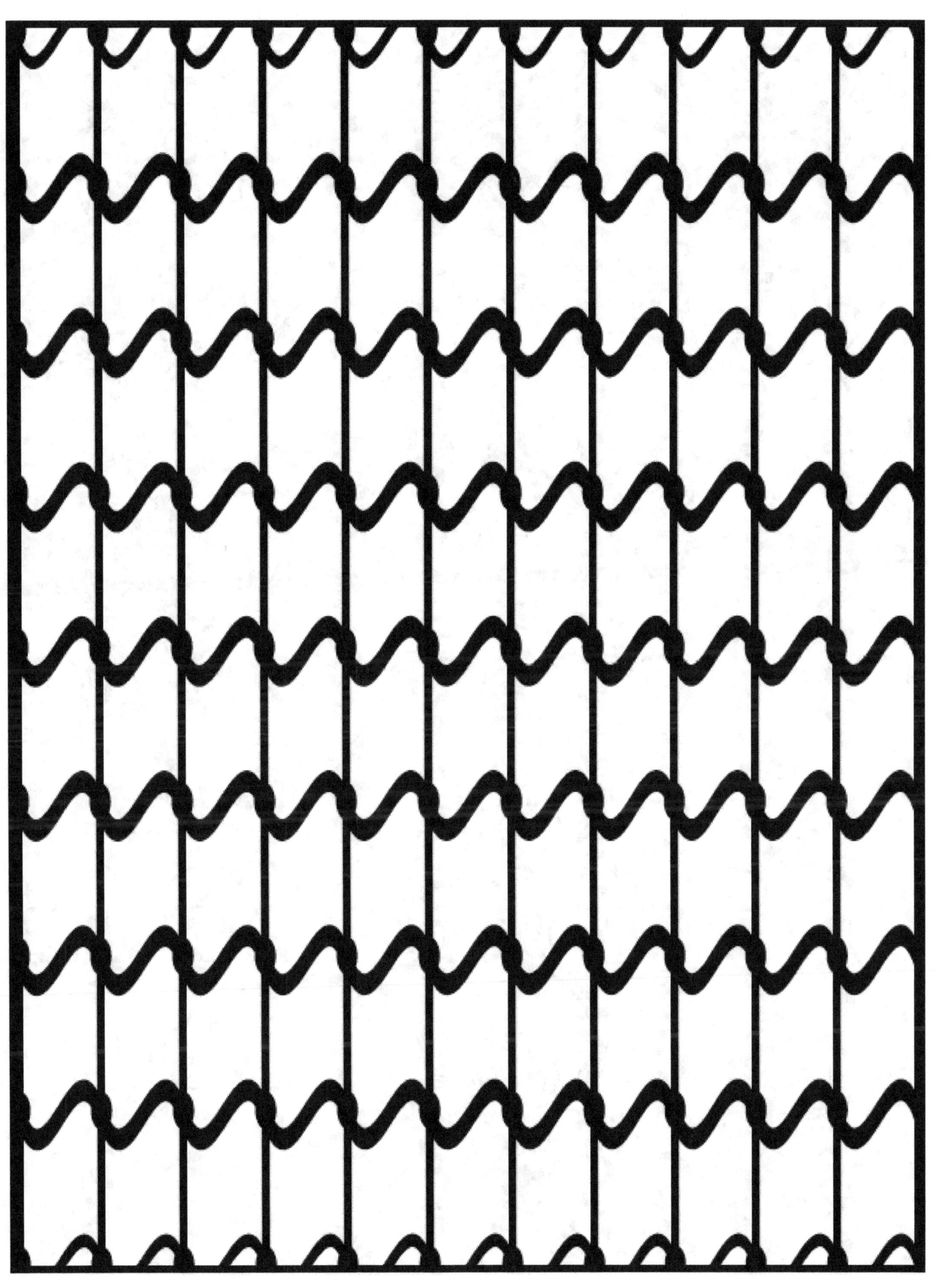

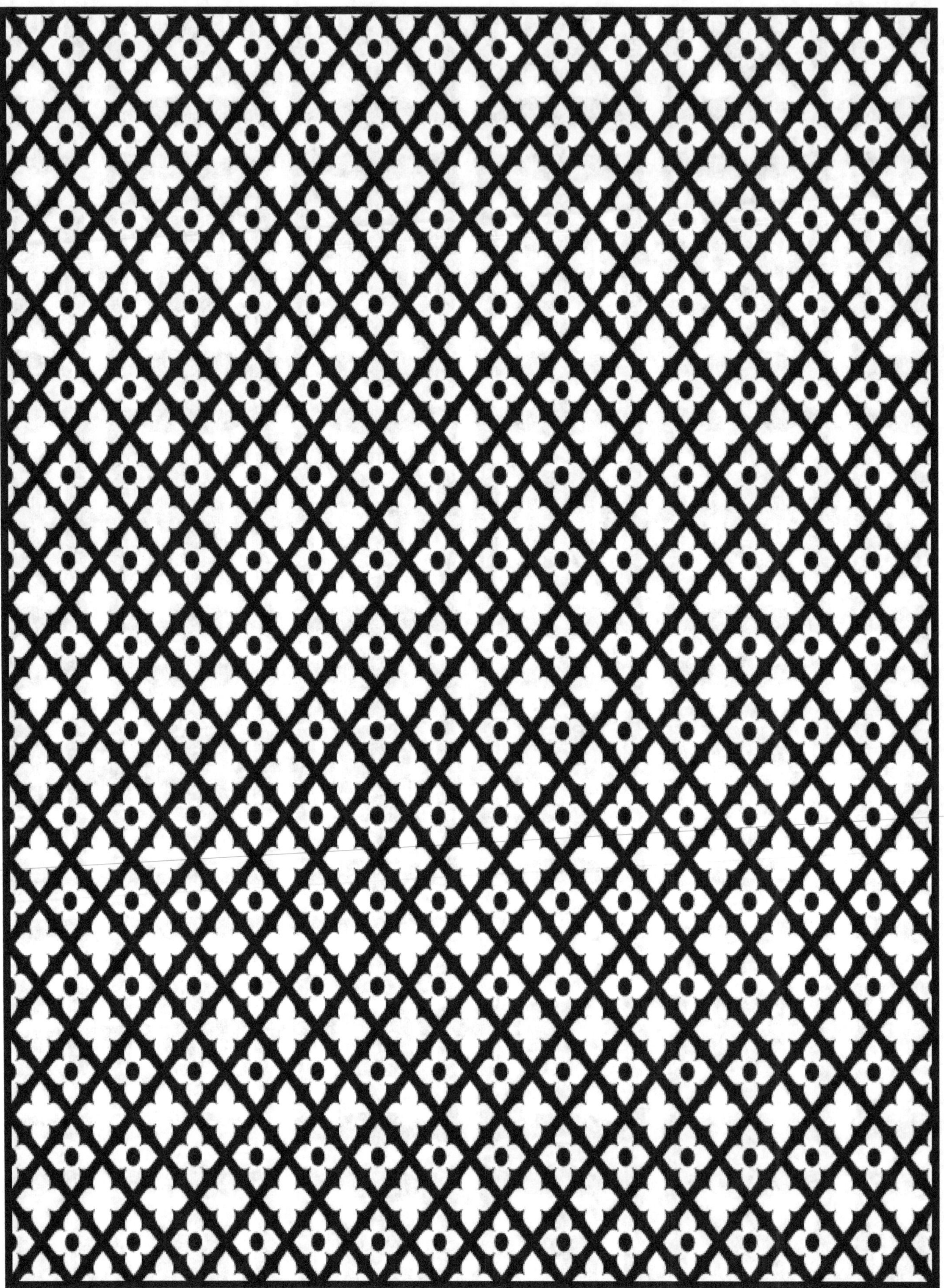